D1538886

I'm In My Feelings Series

OTHER BOOKS BY ROBERT M. DRAKE

Spaceship (2012)
The Great Artist (2012)
Science (2013)
Beautiful Chaos (2014)
Beautiful Chaos 2 (2014)
Black Butterfly (2015)
A Brilliant Madness (2015)
Beautiful and Damned (2016)
Broken Flowers (2016)
Gravity: A Novel (2017)
Star Theory (2017)
Chaos Theory (2017)
Light Theory (2017)
Moon Theory (2017)
Dead Pop Art (2017)
Chasing The Gloom: A Novel (2017)
Moon Matrix (2018)
Seeds of Wrath (2018)
Dawn of Mayhem (2018)
The King is Dead (2018)
What I Feel When I Don't Want To Feel (2019)
What I Say To Myself When I Need To Calm The Fuck Down (2019)
What I Say When I'm Not Saying A Damn Thing (2019)
What I Mean When I Say Miss You, Love You & Fuck You (2019)

For Excerpts and Updates please follow:

Instagram.com/rmdrk
Facebook.com/rmdrk
Twitter.com/rmdrk

ISBN: 978-1-7326900-9-7

Book Cover: Robert M. Drake

For The Ones Who Feel Like They've Lost
Everything

CONTENTS

HOW COULD I	1
LOVE YOU	3
TWITTER	4
NOTHING IS HERE	5
NOT FOR NO ONE	6
SOME YEARS	10
FADE AWAY	13
THE FIRST PERSON	14
FURTHER AWAY	19
NAIVE ENOUGH	20
PEOPLE PLACES & LOVE	23
TOO EARLY TO BREAK	24
SEVERAL YEARS	28
I GET IT	31
A STORM	32
REAL LIFE	33
MEMORIES	34
THE QUESTION	36
MOON SHINERS	40
THE LOUDNESS	44
NO U-TURNS	45
THAT PLACE	46
UNFORGETTABLE	47
MOVEMENT	49
GOOD OR BAD	50
STAY STRONG	52
I SEE YOU	53
THIS!	55
THE DIFFERENCE	56
THE PAST	58
PERSON AFTER PERSON	59
I AM SORRY	62
USED TO BE	63
SADLY	64
TRUST IS	65
YEARS	67
BE ENOUGH	68
YOU DO NOT	69
I KNEW IT	70
NOT WEAK	72
NO ONE IS...	73

FOR MYSELF   75
HOW MANY   78
CLOUSURE   79
A MARK   82
THE MISTAKES   84
YOU AT ALL   88
WHEN YOU CARE   89
FALSE REALITIES   91
WE HURT   93
WHAT PAINS YOU   94
MAKE ME CRY   96
IN THE MIDDLE   97
BAD FOR YOU   98
HARD TO FIND   101
WE STILL TRY   102
BEST ADVICE   105
THE RIGHT PERSON   107
STILL LEARNING   108
SPECIAL TO ME   110
HOW BEAUTIFUL   111
DISCONNECTED   114
FAME AND MONEY   115
YOUR FEELINGS   119
BED OF FLOWERS   120
LOST MYSELF   124
THE TIME   125
OUR SHIT   131
FOLLOW MY HEART   132
MY HEART IS...   135

What I Feel When I Don't Want To Feel

ROBERT M. DRAKE

HOW COULD I

How could I not
be addicted to you.

When all my life
I've been told

you exist.

When all my life
I've been told

to keep searching
for you,

been told
that you've been waiting
for me, too.

So tell me,
how could I not
want to be with you.

How could I not
want to spend every minute

drowning into you,
falling into you,
and find it within me

to put all the pieces back
together again.

So tell me,
with all soul...

that you feel the same way.

Tell me
with all heart

and without contradiction.

Tell me
you need me

just as much
as I need you

and why every moment
we've lived

was meant to bring us closer...
than that

of what we already are.

I just want to love you
without effort.

That's all.

LOVE YOU

I will always love you
because you gave me

all the reasons
I needed

to appreciate myself.

To believe
in what I feel

and live for myself.

And above all,
you gave me all the reasons

to find
and fall in love

with myself again.

I could never repay you
but I could always

thank you for everything
you've done.

Thank you.

TWITTER

A girl on Twitter
makes a post
and tags me in it.

It said,

"Poetry is my religion
and @rmdrk is god."

Please, my love.
Please, my sweet human.

Please, for my own sanity
and yours.

Do not call me a god.

Do not,
I beg of you.

It is blasphemy.

I have yet
to understand
what life is.

I am nothing.

NOTHING IS HERE

Sometimes
you just have to let go.

No matter how much
love you have for them.

Sometimes
you have to find the courage
within you

to move on,
to start over,

and to *hope*
for nothing

but the best
from here on out.

NOT FOR ANY ONE

You don't feel the need
to change when everyone else
is changing.

You don't go through seasons,
through these phases,

although,
you hold the moon
in your hands

and the sun
in your heart.

You stay true
to your feelings.

You stay true
to who you are—to who
you want to become.

You take care
of your well-being,

of your soul,
when the chaos surrounds you.

You know the difference

between
what hurts
and what doesn't

and bravely enough,
you feel them both
at the same time.

You're strong
and I don't just say that

to build your confidence.

I don't just say that
to give you hope.

I say that
because you're exhausted.

We all are.

I say that
because you still have a fight
in you.

This beautiful way
of undoing yourself.

This beautiful way
of collecting who you are.

Especially
under these rough conditions.

You fall apart in such a way
that I could only admire you

as it happens.

You're an angel
searching for her wings.

A bird
searching for the perfect sky.

A dream
searching for the perfect person
to inspire.

And you'll never stop searching,

not until you find it.

You're willing to go through hell
and back

for what you believe in
and you won't change

for anyone.

You stay true

to yourself

no matter how tragic things get.

You go out
and spread love

as long as you have
the heart for it.

You shed tears,
keep your head up high,
and keep it moving…

and that's what makes you

so goddamn beautiful.

SOME YEARS

A friend of mine lost his job.

He gave them 19 years,
can you believe that?

19 whole years
of sweat and blood
and maybe even

tears.

He said he doesn't know
what to do.

He doesn't know
where to pick up again.

Doesn't know
who he now is,

as he has been doing this
for so long

that it was a part of himself.

I told him that life goes on.
That people move on.
That what you once knew

will come back
around again.

People change.
Lovers leave.
Jobs get replaced.
Hearts break.
Children grow.
Wars continue.

And laughter still
floods the street.

19 years.

And sometimes in life
that's how it happens.

You give someone 19 years
of your life.

Of your heart.
Of your soul.

And in an instant
it disappears.

What you once knew
is over

and you are left

with no options

other than
to move on.

FADE AWAY

It hurts
when they slowly
fade away.

When they slowly
lose interest in you.

When they slowly
move on

without telling you
why.

It hurts.

To live with a heart
full of worry

and act
as if it doesn't affect you—

to watch them
severe your veins...

while pretending
it doesn't hurt

at all.

THE FIRST PERSON

The first person
who breaks your heart

will always teach you
the importance of love.

1. People come and go
and only a handful of them

are willing to stay.

So it is best
to give them your promises.

2. You have to go through pain
every once in a while.

That's how it works.

Pain is inevitable.
Pain is relative.

Pain brings people
closer together.

So it is best to give the people
you love your sorrow.

They will make flowers
out of them.

Believe it.

And

3. Somewhere down the line
a revelation will hit you

like a comet
and when it does

you will think of the first time
you got your heart broken.

And the second
and maybe even the third.

And you will finally realize
the importance of it all.

And you will thank them
for the experiences.

And you will finally bring down
your walls

and learn how to move on.

How to forgive.

How to properly heal.

And you will do
all of these marvelous things

but also,
you will never forget the way
they once made you feel.

You will never forget
the slow burn

that

brokenness brings.

And you will
remind yourself of it

every now and then...
and you will do so

to remember
the importance of letting go
and etc.

To remember
why you should never search
for love in the same place
you lost it.

Why you should never
search for love

in the same place
where it left you broken.

That's the importance of love.

Of going through it—to have it
and cherish it…

but also,
to not fall victim

to the same people
and tragedies that made you feel
even more alone.

To not fall victim
to all things

that covered up the sun.

Those lessons are valuable,
therefore,

it is best to learn
as much as you can

and love
as much as you're willing

to get hurt.

Stay strong.

FURTHER AWAY

I don't know
how to give you

want you need
without losing

a part of myself

I know
I will deeply regret.

And I still don't know
how to love you

without

pushing you further away
a little more.

NAÏVE ENOUGH

There are days
when I feel

like leaving it all behind.

Days where I feel uninspired.
Unmotivated to keep going.

I know.

Perhaps,
I'm being over dramatic.

I know.

Perhaps,
I'm being ungrateful
and naive.

It is just.

Sometimes
I feel too damn exhausted
from it all.

Too damn near
the deep end.

I feel
like I am drowning.

I feel
like I am still a small child
looking for something

that isn't even real.

I feel lost.
I feel empty.

Not broken
but too full.

So full
that I don't even know
what to do with all of this

I have inside of me.

If there's a God out there,

then please,
hear me out.

Then please,
take a moment to listen to me.

To what's in my heart.

I'm sad
but I don't even know
why.

I don't even know
what's bothering me.

And I don't even know
how to make it all go away.

If there is a God,
then please,
by all means,

save me.

Save me
from myself

and help me
see the light again.

Because right now...

I feel
like it is all tumbling down.

Save me from what hurts.

That is all I ask.
Amen.

PEOPLE PLACES & LOVE

People.
Places.
Love.

And relationships.

They're there for a little bit
and then

they're gone...

left to burn
through your memories

for a lifetime.

*That's just the way
things are.*

TOO EARLY TO BREAK

Is it too early
to break in the morning.

To fall apart
in your arms

and whisper
what I feel
within your ear.

Is it too early
to tell you I love you.

To tell you
how much you mean to me
in so little time.

Is it too early
to miss you.

To want you
even more.

To rid you
of any sorrow

and show you
how important it is

to be loved.

Is it too early,
my love? Is it?

Too early,
too soon,

to let go.

Too early,
too soon,

to move on.

And too early,
too soon,

to say good-bye.

I love you,
I really do,

but we're nothing more
but a short dream.

Nothing more
but two strangers

falling into a sea
of lost love

and broken interest.

But nonetheless,
I still love you.

I'll still hold you.

I'll still live in this moment
until the very end.

So tell me,
is it too early

to break in the morning.

To fall apart
in your arms

to help me get through
another day.

Is it too early to love?
Too late to love?

Is there still a chance
for us

to place it back
in order.

To start over

and rest our aching
bodies

into each other's arms.

So please, don't say

it's never too late
or too early

to try again.

I am always willing
to give you

what you need.

SEVERAL YEARS

It's been several years now
and sometimes

I wonder
if what we had was real
or not.

Sometimes
my past plays tricks on me.

And I know
some things had to happen
to change me.

To move me.

While other times,
things happen to question
my reality.

Sometimes
I end up betraying myself.

Questioning what I've done.
Who I've been with.

Who I've loved.

Is any of this real?
It's been so long

since I've held someone
in my arms,

too long.

I'm beginning to think
I dreamt it all up.

I'm beginning to feel
that love is just

a moment away
but never close enough

to breathe in
and claim as my own.

And I am gasping.

I am slowly sinking—reaching
for the surface,

for a life I once knew.

Everything is gone
but hope remains.

Everything is lost

but held deeply in our hearts.

And almost
everyone is forgotten,

except the way
some people

made you feel.

I GET IT

I get it.

You have
torn down walls.

You have ended
civilizations.

You have devoured
many lovers

and their dreams.

I get it,
believe me I do.

You are a hurricane,
but to be honest,

I have survived
bigger storms.

A STORM

A storm is coming.

Find shelter
in someone's heart.

Find comfort
in someone's soul

and fire
and warmth
and love.

It's going to rain soon.

You should find
a safe place

before it pours.

REAL LIFE

We haven't met
in real life,

yet

I'm certain
you've seen

and felt
the deepest parts of me.

I'm certain
you've touched my soul

like no one has

ever

done before.

Like I said,
we don't really know each other

but we do know enough
to make us feel

less alone.

MEMORIES

If the memory
of our broken love

is going to linger,

then by all means,
let it stay

within our hearts
forever.

Let it reach us
when our sorrow

fills our souls
to the brim.

Let it never leave.

Let it manifest
whenever we feel the need
to laugh.

To cry.
To smile.
To remember.

Let it stay

within our souls—embedded
within our minds.

Let it reveal itself
when we need it most.

When we feel the need
to break apart.

When we feel the need
to love

a little more.

THE QUESTION

You asked me once
what I wanted to be

when I got older
and I couldn't find

the words back then.

It has been
over twenty years

since the last time
we spoke

and I now understand
what it is

I want to be.

I want...

To be everything ugly
and beautiful.

To be everything hard
and soft.

To be everything tragic

and gentle.

To be everything you want me to be.

To be everything lost
and found.

To be everything that flows
and everything that doesn't.

To be everything that hurts
and everything that has healed.

I want to be everything for you.

So you could hold me
a little longer.

So you could tell me
how much you love me.

Watch me smile
when you say something silly.

Be there for me
when you feel the need to.

I want to be everything.

That's my answer.

I *still* want to be everything
for you and everything for me.

I want to be
the one you run to

when you feel hurt,
scared, or alone.

I want to be
the one you could depend on

when you feel
like breaking apart,

when you feel exhausted,
and when you feel

like falling down.

I want to be
the one who saves you.

The one you could trust.

The one...
who you know

with all your soul

that is willing

to risk it all...
for you.

I just want to be enough
for you.

I wanted
to be enough for you...

but the conclusion is,
I was too late

and it has taken me years
to realize how important

it was
to be there for you,

especially
when you needed me most.

Some people are just harder
to let go of than others.

Some people
are just meant to stay

in our memories
forever.

MOON SHINERS

And the moon shines.

And the wind carries
my sorrow.

And the storm
in my heart

has nowhere to go.

And this love I hold within
feels like it's falling

from the tip
of my mouth.

And it doesn't pain me
to let it go,

it doesn't make me cry
to watch it leave.

This sadness.

This bitter,
infinite darkness.

And the wounds stay raw.

And the emptiness
stays cold, hollow—devouring

the stars within.

And there's something beautiful
about the process.

Something familiar.

Like watching an old friend
come back home.

And I cannot breathe
because I have forgotten

how to.

And sometimes
I feel dead inside...

like an abandon house
set on fire...

like broken windows—letting
in the rain...

like all things lost—in a cycle,
waiting to be found.

I am here.

I am waiting
and I do not know why.

I am still.
I am confused

and the science that makes me
who I am

cannot be understood.

And the ocean roars.
And the love I have

left inside of me
roars.

Too quiet.
Too loud.
Too deep.
Too out of reach.

And the self-doubt.
And the anxiety.
And the depression.

And the feeling of failure
moves higher than before.

The moon shines
and the slow wind

carries my sorrow
and the storm in my heart

still has no place to go.

No place
to call home.

No place to dwell
and fade in.

No comfort from within...

as all chaos does...
when it is born

from the heart.

THE LOUDNESS

It is sad
when you are meant

to be together
and it does not work out,

but it is even sadder
when you know

you are meant
to be together

but you do not have
the courage within

to say
what it is you feel.

NO U-TURNS

You should not
turn your back

on what you love.

You should not
turn your back

on anything

that makes your heart
a little lighter.

Remember this.

Love what you love.

All else is secondary
and always follow

your heart
no matter what.

THAT PLACE

And sometimes
you find yourself

surrounded with the people
you love

and sometimes
you find yourself

feeling even more alone.

If you are not happy
with yourself,

then you are not happy at all.

No matter who you know.
No matter who is around.

Love yourself
at all costs.

No matter who you lose.

No matter who
you are willing

to let go.

UNFORGETTABLE

And the way
we let go

was unforgettable
and oddly

and hard to forget.

Hard to get over,
hard to get under.

Things happen
and they always do

for a reason.

Whether I was in love
or not.

People came
and then

they went.

People arrived
to teach me something.

Something that would sometimes

take years to realize.

I appreciated it
when I got a lot older.

I appreciated people.

The ones I loved.

The ones I had to let go
and the ones who stayed.

It was hard for me
to move on

but in the end
it was all for something.

It was all
to help me grow

and heal.

To help me
move on.

To help me realize
how much I had to lose.

MOVEMENT

It's hard
to keep someone

when the thought
of losing them

stays in your heart

forever.

It's so hard
to hold on

when any moment
they can

let you go.

GOOD OR BAD

No matter
what I go through.

Good or bad.

I know
there will always be

something sad
in me.

Something hard to understand.

No matter who
I fall in love with.

Who I decide
to let go.

There will always be
a part of me

that is missing.

That's what
you left me with...

with a heart

that could barely heal
and a handful of feelings

I could never say
out loud.

STAY STRONG

It only hurts
when you try

to let go.

When you try
to move on.

It only hurts
because it haunts you

and it manifests itself
to remind you

of how the pain
will always be there.

Stay strong.

I SEE YOU

I see you.

You have flowers growing
out of your chest.

Stars glowing
from within your soul.

And tenderness flowing
through your eyes.

You're beautiful, baby...
I see you.

I see and feel
what you're trying to do.

You want to heal
the people you love

by taking their pain
and making it your own.

You want to help them
stand on their own

and let them
make sense of what hurts

without risking

what it is
they truly love
within their hearts.

I see you, baby.

Keep doing you.
Keep saving.
Keep healing.

And above all,
keep loving.

It looks so fucking
good on you.

THIS!

The grass grows
after the rain

and after the pain
and tears

so will you.

THE DIFFERENCE

I'm different now.

Different from who
I was just a second ago.

Different from who
you'll think I am

once I am gone.

Things change.
People fall.

What goes around
comes around.

And with every breath
I am renewed.

With every moment
I am reborn.

I am better now.

Stronger.
Smarter.
Sharper.

And there isn't
a say

in the universe
who could change that.

AMEN.

THE PAST

The past hurts.

It haunts us
in ways

we never thought possible.

It stays with us
and sometimes

it changes us
for the greater good...

while other times
it doesn't.

Other times,
it just drags us

closer to hell.

To what hurts.

That's life.

PERSON AFTER PERSON

You could go through
person after person.

Relationship
after relationship not knowing

what you feel
or what you're looking for.

You can go through life
lost and feeling empty,

sure,
but one day,

and this
I put on my life,

one day,
someone is going to
mend whatever it is

that's broken.

One day,
someone is going to

fill the void,

the darkness with light
and laughter.

One day,
someone is going to make you

fall in love again,
but not just with them,

with your very own
life as well.

And hey,
maybe it won't last forever,

but it will last long enough
to make you appreciate

what it is you have.

Last long enough
to make you realize

how important it is
to love who you are.

So keep your head up.

No one ever goes through life
completely alone.

Everyone has someone—at least
one person to go home to.

One person
to claim as their own

and one person
to help them

figure things out
as they come.

I AM SORRY

And I'm sorry
for a lot of things

but I am not sorry
for caring.

For trying to save
the parts of you

that you gave up on.

And for giving you
the confidence you needed

to be your own hero.

I will never

ever

apologize for that.

USED TO BE

Things won't go back
to how they used to be

but that doesn't mean
that there are

no good times ahead.

Life can still be
as beautiful as it

once was.

It can still
give you flowers

without the need of water

and it can still
take your breath away

without the need
for air.

SADLY

Sadly,
some people only love

when it hurts,

when it's gone,
or when

it's too late.

TRUTH IS

The truth is,
you can go through life

being loved
while hurting people.

You can go through life
being an asshole

(although,
it is not recommended)

and carelessly
breaking other people's hearts.

Hell,
you can even go through life
doing others wrong

for particularly
no reason at all

but when it is all said
and done,

only the people
who love you

will be there.

Only the people
who genuinely care

about you
will forgive you

and give you
as many chances as you need

to make things right.

YEARS

It has taken me years
to realize

that I
solely belong to myself.

That no amount
of attention

or love
can change that

and that
sometimes

I have to hold my own hand
and tell myself

it'll be okay.

BE ENOUGH

I have the courage
to be sad

when I have to
be sad.

To love
when I have to love.

To cry
when I have to cry.

I have the strength
to pick my heart

off the ground
when it feels heavy

and sometimes

that's enough

to get me going.

Enough
to get me off

the ground.

YOU DO NOT

You don't have to
agree with everyone.

If you love something
then love it,

even if you're the only one
who appreciates

its beauty.

Remember,
everything you're looking for

will be found
when no one

is looking.

I KNEW IT

The worst part was,
I knew it.

I understood what I deserved.

I understood my worth
and value.

I understood the magnitude
of things

and how every time
things got darker
and darker.

And still,
I let her back in.

I let her break me down.

I let her convince me
how there was no one else

but her.

And every damn time
too.

Her smile was that
dangerous.

That addicting.

If she was the sun
then I was her earth.

I would gravitate
back toward her.

No matter how far

off

I went.

NOT WEAK

You are not weak
because you care

about them.

You are strong
because you have

the heart to stay
in a place

you know
you don't belong.

NO ONE IS...

No one is ever
quite prepared

for the end.

No matter how much
you anticipate it.

No matter how many times
you've rehearsed it

in your mind.

You never see it coming
until it happens

and you never expect
the emptiness

it makes you feel
until it arrives.

No one ever likes
good-byes

but deep down inside
we all know
it is inevitable.

We all understand
the values
and the lessons

we learn
with letting go.

And we accept
the way things turn out

no matter
who we lose

in the process.

FOR MYSELF

I've been living for myself
for over a year now,

thinking
about myself first...

and doing things
for myself

and what makes me
happy.

And my only regret is...
not doing it sooner.

Not letting go
of those

who never gave
a *fuck* about me

sooner.

Not letting go
of what brought me down

and what brought me pain...
sooner.

Because this year
I've learned

how to forgive myself.

I've learned
how to make peace

with myself
and everything I could
and can't control.

This year,
I feel

like I've finally learned
how to love myself

and I want to apologize
to myself

for taking this long
to realize this.

For taking this long
to let go

and for taking this long
to finally recognize

what matters most.

My life
is my life

and I should live it
for me

and no one else.

Amen.

HOW MANY

How many, honestly?

How many people
do you have to pretend to be.

How many people
do you wish you were.

How many lives
have you gone through.

Lovers,
places,
and memories.

How many?

Until you finally realize

the only person
you should be chasing...

is you.

CLOUSURE

You don't get closure
from people who've done you

wrong.

From people
who've left you

empty,

alone,
and broken.

Sometimes
you have to let
things be.

You have to
leave them

in the past
and move on.

You shouldn't
have to wait

for an apology.

For someone
to come to your aid.

For someone
to help you

make sense
of your hurting.

Sometimes you have to learn
how to move on—on
your own.

Learn
how to hold

your own hand
and take your own advice.

You have to do this
sometimes.

It's a part
of growing up.

I hope you understand
that this pain

isn't forever.

I hope you understand

how beautiful it could all
still be.

Only the truth
can set you free.

A MARK

Leave a mark
on people.

Live for the people
you love

and the people
you don't.

Be kind to them.
Respect them.

Understand them.

Put yourself
in their shoes.

It is not
such a hard thing

to do.

Love
and spread love

and you will receive it
back in return.

That is how
people will remember you.

Do this.

ALWAYS.

THE MISTAKES

And we are suffering
for the mistakes

we've made
but it's okay

to start over.

It's okay
to admit defeat.

To acknowledge
the brokenness.

The emptiness.

The void
we all carry.

We're all in this
together.

Every single
one of us,

therefore,

there is no need

to pretend
to be better.

No need
to hate

and cause each other
more pain.

No need
for this cold isolation.

No need
for this division.

This towering loneliness.

We are all
in this together...

but how many years
is it going to take

in order for us
to understand this.

How much more
can we all take?

We lose
and we lose

and we have lost
so much more

than we can afford to.

And what we weep for
isn't as impactful

as we think it is.

What we die
for causes and movements

that promote no real change.

And what we really want
goes unheard.

The past
is the past

and the future
is the future...

but it does not
have to be so bitter.

It does not
have to wage

so much pain.

We can still be
what we were meant to be.

Still become
who we want to become.

It's still not
too late to start over.

Still not
too late

to love
the way we were meant

to love.

YOU AT ALL

The way you left
made me question

if any of it
was real.

It made me wonder
if I really meant

anything to you.

You just left.
You didn't look away.

You didn't say a word
and you made me feel

as if

I never meant
anything to you

at all.

WHEN YOU CARE

When you care.

It hurts.

There's no other way
to explain it.

It just hurts.

The way you break
is far more intense.

Like watching your soul
shatter

before your eyes
and there aren't enough words

to describe
what it is you feel.

And it's a pain
that clings to the back

of your heart...
no matter how much

you grow

or heal.

It's one of those feelings
that stays with you...

no matter how many

people

you've learned to love
or let go.

FALSE REALITIES

Don't fall into people
with false realities.

People who preach
love

but practice hatred.

People who talk
about positivity

but are putting
their friends down

when they're not around.

People who manipulate
the hearts of those

who genuinely
want to do good.

Keep your eyes open
for people like this.

You see them coming
from afar...

and don't break your own heart
believing

in their words...

it will only cause you
pain

in the end.

WE HURT

We love
as we hurt—with

magic
and a little bit

of tragedy...

at the same
time.

WHAT PAINS YOU

It pains you.

The absence of something
that was once there.

Something
you've known all your life—that

missing piece
that holds it all together.

Yes,
losing someone hurts

like hell,
but what's worse is

losing that part
of yourself

that brings you back
to where you belong.

That part of yourself
that reminds you

of who you are—of
whom you could be.

That's the real tragedy here.

Not losing someone
you once loved.

It's them
taking that piece of you
with them.

That piece
you thought you'd never lose

to only wake up
one day

with it missing—gone,

and lost
forever.

MAKE ME CRY

I just want to understand...
that's all.

What you feel
and how it makes me feel

and why.

I want to accept you
in such a way

no one else has.

I want to not only
be your lover

but your best friend.

I want to understand
what pains you

and make art of everything

that makes you
cry.

IN THE MIDDLE

Sometimes I feel
like I'm in the middle

between

who I want to be
and who I am.

Between

who I'm trying to love
and who I'm running away from.

Between

my past
and my future

and between

the life I dream about

and the life
I know

I'll never have.

BAD FOR YOU

I don't want
to feel bad for you.

I don't want
to feel this terrible

emptiness

for what you've
been through.

For what you've
told me

about your past.

No.
I refuse to.

I want to tell you
that you are still young.

That you can still
pick up

where you left off
regardless

of what has happened.

I want to tell you
that there's still hope.

That there's still
time for you.

Still a chance
for you

to save yourself.

For you
to patch up

any old wounds.

You're stronger than that.
Smarter than that.

You can still
lift your head up high,

face your fears,
and move on.

You can still
heal in ways

you never thought

possible
and you can still

*find your humanity
in all the things*

you love.

HARD TO FIND

It's hard to find love
when people

aren't honest
with themselves.

It's hard to find
a connection

when everyone you meet
is pretending

to be
someone else.

WE STILL TRY

We try so hard
to show the people

around us
that we are not

vulnerable.

That we are tough
and hard

and impenetrable.

That we are fearless
and strong

and sometimes
even cold...

so much
that we forget

how beautiful it is
to be open

with them.

How beautiful it is

to be human
with them.

To be polite,
kind, and gentle.

To be loving,
caring and soft.

We forget
how important it is
to be understanding.

To cry
in front of them.

We try too hard
not to be

these things
but in reality,

this is all
we want from each other.

What we need
from each other,

but sadly,
no one is willing

to make the change
for themselves.

The cycle is never broken.
The love is never revealed.

And what could be,
never happens.

And what hurts
the most is,

most of us
will go through our lives

believing
that this is enough.

Most of us
will go through our lives

believing
we don't deserve

a little more.

BEST ADVICE

Some of the best advice
I ever received

was

"To find someone
who knows

how to bring out
the sun

in the middle
of the storm.

To find someone
who knows

how to make you smile
when you're sad.

And most importantly,
to find someone

who knows
how to make the best
of things

when you feel

like you're beginning
to fall apart."

THE RIGHT PERSON

The right person
will know

what to do
with your love.

You won't feel
the need

to explain
what you want

or deserve.

The right person
will give you

enough

and sometimes
they'll give you
even more.

Stay beautiful,
my friends.

STILL LEARNING

And I've learned
a lot of things

this year
but the most important

thing I've learned is

that with every harsh
good-bye

comes a beautiful awakening.

That

with every door
that closes,

there's another one
opening soon after.

And

whenever you help someone
and genuinely mean it,

the universe crowns you
and grants you

the spiritual growth
you need.

SPECIAL TO ME

You remind me
of all the love

I have for myself.

That is why
you're so goddamn

special to me.

HOW BEAUTIFUL

Imagine how beautiful
it is

to have someone
you can open up to.

Someone
you can trust,

depend on.

Someone
you know

with your gut
that they won't

fuck you over.

Someone
who won't lose you

without a fight.

Who can't see themselves
without you.

Someone

who will need you
just as much

as you will need them.

Imagine
having a best friend,

falling in love
with them,

and going through the fire
together...

hand in hand.

Imagine that,

that could be you.
That could be us.

All you have to do
is open your heart.

Love is two people
existing

in the past
and in the future

and making sense

of it all
in the present.

True love
is friendship

and forgiveness.

Sacrifice
and loyalty.

Both the sun
and the moon

colliding

at the very same
time.

DISCONNECTED

I have to
disconnect sometimes.

Find my own feelings
sometimes.

There's nothing wrong
with our relationship.

I just need
to be

on my own sometimes.

That's all.

FAME AND MONEY

They glorify fame
and money

but fame
and money aren't real.

And hate
and violence

don't stand
for anything.

The real value is
in relationships.

In who you build with.

In who you ride
or die with.

They preach to the youth
the wrong things.

Self-destruction is not beautiful.

Wasting your life away
in drugs

and alcohol
is not heroic.

There's nothing holy
about fucking as many people

as you can—to
glorify it

as if
you've won some kind
of contest.

There's nothing special
in impressing people

who don't like you
to begin with.

There's nothing brave
or courageous

about ignoring those
who really love you.

I know
you are young

and I know
you still have a lot

of life
to live,

a lot
of lessons to learn.

But please,
don't find yourself
in the darkness.

Don't be consumed
by trivial things

and don't follow
trends who offer

so little.

Trends
that don't make

humanity better.

You have
your whole goddamn life

in front of you, babe.

Don't let it slip
through your hands

and don't break your own heart
chasing everything you see.

Your soul is beautiful
but your heart

is the most precious thing
in the world.

Protect it.
Protect your magic

at all costs.

YOUR FEELINGS

Search your feelings.

Don't be afraid
to question yourself

and never keep doing so

until you receive
what you deserve.

BED OF FLOWERS

Your mind is a bed
of flowers.

A garden
of roses

and dandelions.

Your soul is
as old as

a river.
A tree.

The sun
and the moon.

Breathing.

Inhaling the freedom
of the gods

and exhaling
the seeds of life

into the middle
of your soul

where gold is found.

I love you now
and I'll love you then.

But good-byes
are harsh to say.

And meaningful ones
are hard to come by.

Your body is earth.

Where your feelings
are grown,

harvested,
and shared.

Handle it with care.

You are soft.

You are more
than just flesh and bone.

You are more
than just a human.

More
than what you can

imagine.

More
than whatever

washes toward
the shore.

Your mind is a bed
of flowers

and your soul
is a star

and your body
is the shell

but your heart
is what governs them all.

It is
what keeps you going.

What keeps the rest
of your parts in order.

The heart.
The human heart.

The only thing known
to break

and keep going.

To be ripped out
and still keep you alive.

This heart.
This pain.
This love.

It is everything
and you owe it

to yourself
to know

what you're living for.

What you're dying for.

The truth is
not only out there

but it is also
within you.

LOST MYSELF

I almost lost myself
doing things for others.

The year is almost gone
and I'm

just learning this.

I have to move forward
for me.

I have to find
what makes me happy

for me.

And

I have to learn
how to live,

ultimately,
for me.

THE TIME

It's one a. m. now
and this is the time

it usually begins
to hurt.

The time
I begin to feel it most.

This is the time
it all reverts

from the beginning.

From the moment
I met you

to the moment
I last saw you.

It hurts
and it feels like my life

is slowly walking out
of my body.

As if
my breathing

is slowing departing
from me.

It's two a. m. now
and whatever I was feeling before

has now
settled in.

I can feel it
in my bones.

I can feel it
beneath my skin.

Beneath my chest,
filling my heart

with emptiness.

With numbness.

At this point
it doesn't hurt.

It becomes something else,

something
I can't put into words.

Flashbacks flash.

Memories fade in
and out.

The playback.
The reversal of time.

Of you.

All in my head.
All within my reach.

I close my eyes
and the shore washes

my regret.

What I should have done

instead

of what has been done.

The sorrow follows.
Like a cloud pouring

and pouring
and pouring.

It's over.

It really is.

I never thought
it would happen

but it did.

Something always told me
to keep my guard up.

To get close
but also, keep my distance.

To look out
for myself

more than anything else...

but I didn't.

I never have
and now

in conclusion,
here I am,

a broken man.

A broken lover...
searching for whatever is left

of me.
For whatever

is left of us.

It stops.

It ends,
as all good things do.

And the pain
is continuous

but every so often
I get a good night in-between.

It hurts,
as I mentioned.

And my soul
has become a hallway.

A haven
for all lonely things...

You are
all safe here.

You are all
loved here.

It's three a. m. now
and I laugh
and I inhale

a little more

and

as the seconds
fly by me,

I think I'm falling apart.

*Holding on
is a motherfucker.*

OUR SHIT

We talk our shit.

We argue,
get mad,

and sometimes

barely agree
on anything.

But I always
come back to you.

We know
where we belong.

And we both know
how to find our way

back home.

FOLLOW MY HEART

I would pretend
not to give a fuck

when you would text me.

I would forward
your calls

when you needed me
the most.

I purposely
chose my friends

over you...

time
and time again.

And for what?
To prove what?

That I'm a sucker for love?

That I'm too hard
to keep it real with you?

That I'm too afraid

to be vulnerable.

Too afraid
to show you

what I feel...

or was it
to hurt you

before you hurt me.

What was it all for?

To lose you.
To cry alone
over you.

To regret
all the bullshit

I ever did to you.

In the end,
I did this to myself.

I caused you
so much pain

but when it was all
said and done...

the only person
I was hurting

was myself.

Damn.

Growing up is hard.
Making it work
is hard

but nothing is harder
than accepting

the past
and finally realizing

how it all
could have been avoided...

if only
I followed my heart.

MY HEART IS...

My heart
is made of solid gold

and yet,
you have decided
to ignore it.

You have chosen
not to acknowledge
my value

and for that
I say

these two magic words:

"fuck off"...

because I know
my worth

and maybe one day
you'll know yours, too.

Maybe one day
you'll see things

for what they really are

and not

for what you
think they are.